Men Hurt Too!

By Levon Sparks Salone

Kindle Edition 2014

Copyright©2014 Levon Sparks Salone

Names, occupations, ages, and other personal information of the interviewees have been changed to protect their identities.

Other Books by Levon Sparks Salone

Fiction:

Waltzing With Deception (The Chillings Series, Book 1)

Unjust Ruling (The Chillings Series, Book 2)

Non-Fiction:

Writing Prompts for Creative Writers

Introduction

I decided to write this book because information about hurting men is very limited. Women readily talk about their hurts and pains; however, most men hide their feelings (especially if they have been hurt emotionally). Society instructs them to "take it like a man," "don't be a sissy," and "don't ever let them see you cry." These instructions sound valiant; however, they build walls within men that are rarely broken down. It became obvious to me (in various counseling sessions and encounters with men) that men hurt too. Because of this discovery, I decided to interview men from different walks of life. I wanted to tell their stories.

My desire is that this book will help every hurting man. No, you may not find your exact experience in this book, but you may identify similar feelings, spoken from the lips of other men who have experienced hurt or are currently hurting. I suggest you put your seatbelts on men! We're getting ready to explore: **Men Hurt Too!**

And ladies, before the men take this journey, make yourselves available for the man in your life (whether he's your husband, son, father, uncle, boyfriend, etc.) if he desires to talk about his feelings regarding this book. Don't lecture, try to solve his problems or try to identify with his pain. Just listen. And yes, get this book for every man you know (both young and old). It will be money well spent.

Suggestions For The Use Of This Book

To discuss each situation in Men's Fellowship Meetings (Men's Breakfasts, Men's Ministries, Men's Informal Meeting Groups, and with Prayer Partners).

To discuss feelings with the female in your life (share how you identify with the interviewees).

To identify areas in which you may need (or desire) personal counseling (areas that bring up strong feelings may be areas that need to be processed further in some type counseling format).

To identify personal areas for change (through journaling, accountability to others, goal setting, etc.)

How to Use This Book

For Group Discussions:

Read one story per session. One person can read the story aloud or each participant can read the story silently.

Have someone read each question. Allow each participant to give his answer.

Or

Assign one story for homework assignment. Have men write down answers then discuss answers when they return to group.

For Journaling:

Read each story and write answers in your journal. Discuss with mentor or special person in your life.

Or

Read each story and write answers in your journal. You may choose not to share answers with anyone.

For Sharing with Mate (or Special Person):

Read each story then answer each question. You may ask for feedback from listener if you choose.

Important Notes:

You may need to contact a professional if you have strong feelings about any topic. This is only a tool. Please use a professional to properly diagnose and treat issues.

Questions used during the interviews are included in the back of this book.

Table of Contents

Chapter One

Charles, a fifty-four-year-old business executive, dashes off daily to his elaborately designed office. He makes major decisions for hundreds of employees. He is outgoing, polished, articulate and ambitious. Everyone respects his brilliant wit and business savvy. On the outside, Charles appears to have it all together. Women adore him. Men attempt to imitate him. Some even envy him.

This is the face Charles wears for the business world. However, no one knows what Charles is really like. He has not allowed anyone into his inner circle to see and experience the "real him." In this book, he took a risk to share his "real self" with countless men to expose the man behind the business face.

Charles Speaks:

I grew up in a prominent family. My father worked extremely hard, and my mother stayed home to raise the children. She was always there when we came home from school. She stressed getting a good education so we could obtain respectable careers. My father took time with us, especially on Saturdays, being involved in our sporting events:

football, baseball, soccer, etc. He encouraged us to do our best. To me, life was wonderful. I could not have imagined life being any other way. I had lots of friends, plenty of toys, my parents' attention, loving siblings and community support. Shortly thereafter, my life would change forever.

At the age of ten, my parents allowed me to go to my first summer camp with my baseball coach and teammates. We spent two nights out-of-town, chaperoned by fathers of the team members. Unfortunately, my father couldn't attend this particular weekend because he was working out-of-town. He and my mother reluctantly allowed me to go with the team (after much pleading on my behalf).

Our first day at camp was wonderful. We played games, told jokes, ate good food and did lots of other fun stuff. That night, we tucked ourselves into our bunks, and lights were out by ten.

Approximately two hours after lights were out (according to the big clock on the wall), I had to potty. I ran to tell my dorm leader. Through a woozy stare, he instructed me to go outside in the woods (which were close by), do my business and return to my bunk. A little shaken, I proceeded towards the woods. As I proceeded, I heard an unnerving rustling of leaves. I slowly, yet cautiously, moved closer to my destination with wide-opened eyes. To my relief, it was one of the other dorm leaders smoking a cigarette. He called me over to him. Since he wasn't a stranger, I readily complied. He told me he would keep an eye on me while I did what I had to do. That sounded logical, so I proceeded with my mission.

He went and quickly scanned the area. A few minutes later, he returned and beckoned me to be extremely quiet and still. He had such a bizarre look on his face that I felt compelled to obey. I thought he saw something scary. This frightened me even more. There I was in the midst of a potty session, afraid to move, afraid to even blink an eye. The dorm leader tip-toed to me and began molesting me. (I will never forget that moment as long as I live.) I immediately became numb. I couldn't speak, cry or move. Whenever he finished, he insisted I keep silent about the entire ordeal. He said my parents would send me to a boys' home if they found out I had been so naughty.

When I came to myself, I ran back to my dorm like a crazed animal. The tears wouldn't stop flowing. My dorm leader couldn't understand why I was so hysterical. He tried to calm me but couldn't. I woke up the other boys with my deep yelping. Finally, after an hour of non-stop crying, I ran out of tears. The other boys were afraid, and the dorm leader didn't know what to do. He insisted that he call my parents. I hysterically begged him not to. I told him I was sorry for being naughty and would never do it again. I lied and told him I thought I heard a wild animal coming after me. With that, I went to my bunk and covered my head. For the rest of the trip, I didn't play, talk (unless prompted) or eat. My world had completely changed. I knew within my heart I would never be the same.

From that night on, I carried this secret with me. This was my secret, my sick secret; a secret that haunted me for years to come.

I was never the same after that incident. I became non-caring, moody, distant and pushy. My parents didn't know what happened. They called the coach to see whether anything unusual occurred while I was on the trip. The coach told them I thought I saw a wild animal one night and became hysterical. He said the dorm leader calmed me down, and that was the end of the story. I went along with the lie. How could I ever tell my parents that a man (one whom I knew well) touched my private parts? They would definitely send me to a boys' home, just like he (my perpetrator) said. It's a funny thing, my perpetrator stopped working with the team after that. He told the coach his schedule was too hectic.

Anyway, I started to hate myself. I lost all interest in girls. (I felt dirty around them.) I began to eye boys smaller and younger than me. Somehow, I became preoccupied with them. Approximately a year after the molestation, I molested two little boys (ages three and four). They were too young to tell. I gave them candy and told them it was all part of our secret game.

As the years passed, I became obsessed with males. I kept my obsession to myself because I felt dirty. To combat my negative feelings, I excelled in school. I also excelled in sports. I had to make others think I was okay even though I despised myself.

In my adult years, I worked in the business arena. I pushed for number one in my line of work. No goal was too high. No quest was too much to conquer. I learned how to manipulate with words, telling others what I desired for them to hear but always keeping them at an emotional distance. I could not afford for anyone to know about my struggle. It's still very hard to admit. I'm struggling with homosexual tendencies. I hate myself for it, but I can't control my urges. Like an animal being lured to his death, I am lured to other men. No one can know. What would they think of Mr. Business Executive (the biggest giver in my church), struggling with homosexuality? No, I just can't tell anyone. In fact, this is the first time I exposed the secret (and I only did it because no one can figure out my identity).

Yes, I hurt. I've always wanted a family, but I would never bring a woman into my world and hurt her that way. Many of my sexual partners are men with families, and they play the game well. I just couldn't ever bring myself to live in that level of deception. Now you have it, my secret.

I am still struggling with this, and because of this interview, I have decided to seek counseling. Just exposing this horrific secret has made me feel lighter. I am really hoping to get my life back. Even though I have been successful, I have merely existed. This secret has destroyed the most intimate part of my life.

Charles' Advice:

Don't hold on to your secrets like I did. It ruined forty-four years of my life. If I had sought help earlier, maybe I would have a wife and children. I'm not healed. As a matter of fact, I am just deciding to get help. My hope is that I can get my life back, the life that a grown-up stole from me at the age of ten (during summer camp).

Thought Provokers

What issue was Charles dealing with?

Why do you think he kept his struggle a secret?

Do you think Charles' actions were in conflict with his values? Explain. How do you think he felt about this?

What would you advise Charles to do if he came to you with his secret?

How is Charles' issue affecting his life?

Can you identify with Charles? Explain.

Do you believe men have safe, confidential places to discuss a situation like this? Explain.

Chapter Two

Raymond, a twenty-one-year- old college student, is shy and reserved. He studies excessively and likes the campus scene. Raymond has had many relationships (some platonic, some intimate) with the opposite sex. Wherever he goes, he attracts women. He rarely has to ask women out because most of them desire his company. He's muscular, 6'2", dark and extremely handsome. Not only is he physically attractive, his soft-spoken, soothing mannerisms make him even more appealing.

Raymond's parents raised him in a strict Pentecostal atmosphere where they stressed the sanctity of life. He believes God created all men in His image. During most of his life, Raymond obeyed his parents and did his best to live morally (before he entered college).

Raymond decided to speak to men, hoping his experiences would help some hurting man.

Raymond Speaks:

It was my first day on the college campus. I was among a hybrid of students: freshmen, sophomores, juniors and seniors. I found myself pushing through a haven of ethnic groups, trying to find my first class. In my haste, I bumped into one of the most beautiful creatures on God's green earth. (I didn't know it at the time, but I would end up dating this lovely creature in my sophomore year.) I apologized for my unintentional rudeness and continued on my way. I thought about this beautiful creature for the rest of the day then thoughts of her faded into my subconscious.

I must admit, my freshman year was wonderful. I made lots of friends (even though I was shy) and was very active with the campus news group. I didn't remember running into this beautiful creature again in my freshman year, even though thoughts of her frequently danced across my mind.

Approximately two months into my sophomore year, I saw a scene that made me stop in my tracks. There she was again, the most beautiful creature on God's green earth. There, standing at the water fountain was the girl of my dreams. I decided not to allow her to get away this time. I introduced myself and asked permission to walk her to class. Just being in her presence made me feel like a blessed angel.

We continued to spend time together (Dessie and I), and for the first time in my life, I was in love. I told Dessie about myself, inside and out. She did the same with me. We went beyond our boundaries and became physically intimate. Because we both came from strict Pentecostal backgrounds, we knew what we were doing was wrong, but oh, did it feel so right.

About six months into the relationship, Dessie said she had something to tell me. She suggested we skip classes that day. This was out of character for Dessie because she was so studious. Being that it appeared urgent, I agreed. As we walked through the private outskirts of the campus, Dessie, through tears, told me she was pregnant. Pregnant? I could barely believe what I was hearing. I held her as she wondered what she would do. She was nineteen, and I was twenty. And here we were, going to have a baby. I tried to comfort Dessie and told her I would be with her through this ordeal. She looked at me through tear-stained eyes and announced that she was thinking about getting an abortion. Appalled, I told her she could never kill our baby, a baby conceived through love.

Dessie ran off, and I didn't hear from her for a week. She went, without my agreement or consent and had an abortion. Three weeks after she informed me of the pregnancy, she presented me with a bill (a bill for an abortion). I was devastated. We didn't talk; we just hugged and cried.

Things were never the same between Dessie and me afterwards. After about a year into the relationship, we broke up. The pain was unbearable. We both had recurring nightmares. We both cried a lot.

I finally told my parents. They were disappointed, but they said they, as well as God, still loved me. They did not condone my actions, but they prayed with me to help me through the pain.

As for Dessie, she left school. She would not accept my telephone calls. She returned my letters unopened. She blocked my email address from her computer. Talking about pain! My first love ended in disaster. During that time, I experienced pain I wish on no man.

Since Dessie, I can't commit to another woman. As soon as a woman gets close, I run. Regardless of how good she is, I get afraid. I'm still afraid. Will I ever commit to one woman again? Well, I pray, and I believe God to heal me of the pain.

Raymond's Advice:

If you love a woman, marry her before having sex with her. The pain of abortion is too great to bear. I know they say women are the only ones who suffer because of this, but I'm here to tell you, men suffer too.

A part of me died when Dessie had that abortion. I often wonder whose eyes our baby would have had. If the baby were a girl, would she have been beautiful like her mother? If a boy, would he have taken on my personality? I will never find the answers to these questions in this life.

As for getting help, I didn't choose counseling; I chose to allow God to heal me through His Word. I see myself getting better day by day. As for Dessie, I still pray for her.

Thought Provokers

What issues are Raymond dealing with?

Why do you think these situations hurt him so badly?

What feelings do you think Raymond is experiencing?

How are these situations impacting Raymond's life now?

What could Raymond have done differently to prevent these situations?

What advice would you give Raymond?

Can you identify with Raymond? Explain.

Do you think men struggle with their mates having abortions? Explain.

Chapter Three

Jerome, a thirty-five-year-old gangster type, took pride in being "the man." People jumped at his command. He commanded respect as he entered a room, and for those who didn't follow suit, he demanded it from them. He always had on thousands of dollars of jewelry, sporting the latest in fashion designs. Everywhere he went, he had a woman on each arm. It was nothing for him to go through women like he went through clothes. All Jerome knew were "the streets." Big money, fast money, fast cars, beautiful women, fancy foods and fast living were synonymous with his name.

At the time of the interview, we find Jerome behind bars in a tightly secured prison. He had been there for a year, serving a seven-year sentence after getting caught in a drug bust in which a few of his close associates ratted on him to save their own necks. Instead of sporting the latest fashions, Jerome was sporting a prison uniform. There was nothing fancy about his living quarters, just the bare necessities in a bar and stone surrounded space.

Jerome agreed to reveal bits and pieces about himself to help other men.

Jerome Speaks:

I ain't really into this interviewing "thang," but I will help a sister girl out who is trying to help out the brothers. I'm really private you know, and I don't usually put my business in the streets. But you seem like a good girl, so I will help out the cause.

Me, I was born in the projects. Yep, the projects in the big city. Never knew my old man. My mom whored with every man that had legs. She said she had to support the family. Men would always come around drinking and doing dope. Me and my brother saw some strange _____ (you know, stuff). I would make him go to bed when the men came. I didn't want that junk poisoning his mind. I would lay in the next bedroom, hating the place. Hating the man that gave up his sperm to birth me, hating my whoring mom. Just hating everything. I promised my brother that I would get him out of that hell hole some day.

At the age of twelve, I started to hang out with the rough neighborhood kids. We stole from the corner store, robbed old people and beat up kids. We took their shoes, clothes, money or anything else they had that we wanted. I would shield my brother from this because he respected me as his big bro.

By the age of fourteen, I was selling drugs big time. I had my own little posse, and they were my runners. I would organize the business, and they would bring me the loot. If anybody tried to stiff me, I would make a public example of him. I developed quite a reputation, and the name "J Dawg" stuck with me. (People knew they would get dogged if they messed with Jerome.)

As my mom grew worse (with the alcohol, drugs and men), I became more angry. I would make my runners work harder and give them less pay. I started to run the women like never before. I was obsessed with becoming a great drug lord (at any expense). I insisted that my brother move in with my grandma in the south because I didn't want him in the madness. I would shoot, cut, con and so forth, to get what I wanted. My feelings grew numb, and I was on a mission: destroy before getting destroyed.

Everything was going as planned until a few of my home boys ratted on me. They planned things so smoothly. I still don't know who did it, but the word is out that it was somebody from my camp.

Let me let you in on the low down. It was a Thursday night, and my runners brought in a lot of loot (more than usual). I should have known something was wrong because Yellow Man was a little nervous. He always seemed a little strange, but he was one of my best producers. I questioned him unmercifully that night. He assured me that everything was on the up and up. I promised to blow his brains out if he was lying. My instincts told me to be watchful, but I guess I let my guard down when I saw all of the money Yellow Man brought in.

As I was counting my cash, there came a knock on the door. I pulled out my piece, but it was the code so I eased up. In walked one of my "dawgs."

When I saw him, I put my piece down and went back to counting my cash. Just as I did, the feds busted in the door and yelled that we were under arrest.

They threw me, Yellow Man and "my dawg" to the floor. They handcuffed all three of us and took us to jail. It was a long, drawn out process, but Yellow Man and "my dawg" got released. I was sent up the creek. So, here I am, in the pen.

You asked me have I ever been hurt. Well, how would you feel if you saw every man in the projects sleeping with your mom? The more I saw, the angrier I got. I'm not blaming my life on my old lady or my old man. I made this choice. I'm just saying that was no life for a kid to have to live. How do I deal with this? I use and abuse anybody that comes in my path. That's just how it is in this world, the drug world. Do I regret what I did? Heck no! I had to escape that life of poverty and slinging dope was my hope. Maybe something will happen while I'm in the pen to change my mind. Who knows?

Jerome's Advice:

(Jerome raps something similar to a beat)

Hating on my mama
And my old man
My entire life, you see.
Said I didn't need 'em
Needed no one
In this big, old world but me.
Started slinging dope
For it was my hope
But my hope done let me down.
Deal with your stuff man
Before it's too late
To turn your life around.

Note: *Jerome said he has a lot of time to think while incarcerated. He hasn't made a decision on which route to take, but he definitely wants the "little Jeromes" to think before they take the route that he took.*

Thought Provokers

Why do you think Jerome was hurting?

How did Jerome cover his pain?

Name others who may have gotten hurt because of Jerome's pain.

What advice would you give Jerome?

Can you identify with Jerome? Explain.

What do you think would have to happen for Jerome to change his life?

Chapter Four

Lewis, a thirty-eight-year-old stockbroker, celebrated ten years of marriage. When asked about himself, he talks about his wife first. He said God used her to help him become the man he is today. He feels his wife is a blessing from God.

Lewis was born and raised in the rural South. There were ten children in the family, and he was the oldest son. Being responsible was a requirement. The women, however, were the dominant ones in his family. He watched his great-grandmother, grandmother and mother take on huge tasks and fulfill their roles. He learned from observation that a man supplied the bacon, and the woman ruled the nest.

When Lewis tried to voice his opinions, his father told him to run things by his mother. As a child, Lewis felt that advice was fine; however, as he approached adolescence and adulthood, he wanted to think independently. As he tried to take a more active role in his life, his mother became more domineering. She used guilt tactics to silence him and make him conform to her whims. Inside, Lewis developed resentments. He masqueraded total agreement with his mother, but inwardly felt continuous hostility towards his parents: hostility towards his father because he saw him as weak and hostility towards his mother because he saw her as domineering. He vowed to move out on his own as soon as he could and never marry a woman like his mother. He also promised not to follow his father's example.

Lewis moved out of his parents' house at the age of twenty-five. A few years later, he met and married Karen. Lewis was automatically attracted to Karen. Something about her felt familiar; he knew she was the one for him.

Lewis shared how his life transitioned after this point. He hopes that through his sharing, some man will get help if he needs it.

Lewis Speaks:

Meeting and marrying Karen were the best things that ever happened to me (so I thought). In the beginning, Karen was very attentive and loving. I knew she was quick-tempered, but I bought her small tokens to show my love, and that always calmed her. I used to call her outbursts "little love spats."

After our marriage, the "little love spats" became more volatile, especially if I didn't do as Karen demanded. To keep the peace, I neglected what I wanted and conformed to her wishes. Initially, I didn't realize the connection. It seemed that I lived these scenes before, but I couldn't picture where. Finally, after a frustrating bout with Karen, it hit me. I married my mother! I smiled on the outside to appease Karen, but inwardly, I seethed with anger. How could I be so deceived? I vowed never to marry a domineering woman. I vowed never to turn out like my father, and there I was, reliving the same pattern from generations before.

As Karen grew more demanding, I withdrew. I lied about my whereabouts. I told her I would be working late, and I would end up at the bar, fingering a drink. I didn't want the liquor; I just didn't want to go home.

One night while on one of my avoidance sprees, I met Cassandra. Cassandra was sweet, sassy and a great listener. She sympathized with my situation. After a long conversation, she gave me her number just in case I needed a friend. My first instinct told me to throw the number away, but I kept it for when I needed to talk to someone. I knew for sure I couldn't talk to Karen. The only thing I would get from her was a lecture.

It was weeks before I returned to that bar. But when I did, I saw a smiling Cassandra, looking just as gorgeous as she did the first time I met her. She bought me a drink and motioned for me to sit at her table. Since that wasn't a crime, I joined her.

I was disgusted with Karen. Every word that came out of her mouth was a command. How did it get to that point? I directed my question towards Cassandra (as if she would know). She listened intently, held my hand, and comforted me with her words. That night, I did something I thought I would never do. I was unfaithful to my wife. I stepped out on Karen.

After the incident, I rationalized my behavior. I told myself that Karen deserved it because she tricked me into marrying her. If she had only shown me her true colors, I would have never proposed to her. If she would listen to me, I would have never turned to Cassandra. If, if, if.

I saw Cassandra off and on for six months. One night, without my knowledge, Karen followed me in her friend's car. She saw me going into Cassandra's apartment. She waited four hours until she saw me stand to leave. She met me at Cassandra's door as I turned the lock. I thought my life would end right in that spot. I tried to explain, but she left without saying a word. I didn't go home that night. I rode around in a daze. When I did get home, I found Karen packed and gone. My heart almost stopped. At first, I thought I wanted out of the marriage, but when it became a reality, I panicked. I realized that the woman whom I truly loved had exited my life. I wept all day. I didn't bathe, eat, sleep or go to work for a week. I was devastated.

I didn't hear from Karen for at least three months. I was a nervous wreck. There were so many things I wanted to say to her. So many things I wanted to apologize for. So many things I wanted to do for her. It was now too late. Too late to make amends. At that point, I fell on my knees and cried out to God. I told Him I would do anything to get my wife back. I told Him I would become a better person if He would answer this prayer for me.

After my prayer, another month rolled along. Still no Karen. Then one day out of the blue, she showed up on my doorsteps. She looked wonderful, but I was a living wreck. I lost weight, my hygiene was poor, and the house was a mess. I was surviving, and she looked as if she was really living. She wanted to talk. I apologized for the mess and invited her in. We discussed everything under the sun that day. I know we talked non-stop for four hours. Karen informed me that she had been in counseling for at least two months. She apologized for belittling me. She felt she chipped away at my manhood (sometimes intentionally and sometimes unintentionally).

She forgave me for the affair. That day, I shared my heart with Karen. We discussed my childhood, my resentments, my fears and the affair. I cried uncontrollably in her lap. It was the best cry I ever had in my life.

After the conversation, Karen requested that I attend counseling with her. I agreed (basically because I was at a point of desperation). I tell you, it was one of the best things we could have done for ourselves and our marriage. We both worked through a lot of pain. We finally learned how to communicate with each other instead of talking at each other. To this day, I can say that Karen is my best friend. I don't have to go outside of the marriage to get my needs met. Karen has me thoroughly covered in that department. (He smiles.)

Lewis' Advice:

Counseling is not a bad thing. Sometimes you have to shake off that male ego in order to get the help you need. I almost lost the love of my life because I was too manly to share my pain. Believe me; help is available if you want it. Get it before it's too late.

Thought Provokers

List the issue(s) you think Lewis was dealing with.

What situation in Lewis' childhood spilled over into his adult life?

In what unhealthy ways did Lewis deal with his frustrations?

If you had been as frustrated with your mate as Lewis was with Karen, what would you have done?

Can you identify with Lewis? Explain.

What do you think Karen learned from this entire ordeal?

Do you think a marriage can survive an affair? Explain.

Chapter Five

Luther is a forty-five-year-old dynamic preacher who has preached for the last twenty years; he sees it as the love of his life. Luther oversees a growing and vibrant congregation, and most of his members say they love the Word of God. Luther encourages his members to excel in the Power of the Lord.

Luther is also a dedicated husband and father. He married Suzanne five years ago, and they have two sons (ages one and three). Luther is very conscientious about his family life. Even though he loves being a pastor, he spends one day per week solely with his family. He feels if a man wants a happy home, the queen of his house, as well as his children, must receive quality time.

Luther decided to share his past struggles so that men can see that freedom is an option.

Luther Speaks:

I have not always loved God as I do now. As a child, I hated going to church. It was boring. We could not talk, laugh, play or write notes in church. We had to listen to the same old uninteresting preacher and the same old spiritless choir every

Wednesday night and Sunday morning. They didn't have a youth program in my church back then. It seemed that the youth motto was: be seen and not heard. Nevertheless, my mom insisted that as long as we had breath, we had to attend church.

I was basically a good kid, always curious. I never got into any real trouble, just the routine boyish pranks. I skipped the drinking and drugging scene, and basically made my parents proud.

I didn't get married until age forty; I married a beautiful woman (inside and out), and later, fathered two sons. As I recall, I accepted the call into the ministry years before I married, so the sisters of the church were always trying to set me up with the proper wife. They said it didn't look good for a man of God to go without his helpmeet. Thank goodness Suzanne came along when she did. She was perfect for me, and it stopped the sisters from invading my personal life.

Due to advanced technology, I spent a lot of time on my computer: developing and maintaining the church website, searching for ministering materials, emailing brethren in the Lord, etc. During my time online, I received triple X advertisements. I deleted them and went on about my business.

One night, while checking the flow of traffic to our church website, I received a pop-up: a triple X pop-up. I scanned the contents. I told myself it really couldn't hurt because I was only going to browse the site. Besides, who would know? As I sat battling the issue in my mind, my curiosity got the best of me. I gave in and pulled up the site. Instead of a brief glance, I spent an hour there. The things I saw were shocking, yet intriguing. Ashamed at my interest in this site, I hesitantly continued my perusal. I experienced an immediate rush from the experience.

Week after week, I went from a few minutes of glancing to hours of lusting. I recalled how I turned on my computer with the intent to study for my sermons and ended up spending hours on a porn site. How could this happen to me? A man of the cloth? A man who loves God?

Things started to deteriorate right before my eyes. My relationship with my wife became strained. My children became unruly. My sermons were no longer anointed. (I basically went through the motions.) And the scariest part of all, I lost vision for the church. I became consumed with lust. I didn't actually become physically intimate with anyone else, but mentally and emotionally, I developed a relationship with the porn sites.

Suzanne threatened to leave me if I didn't get help. She said she felt like I didn't love her anymore because of my obsession with those sites. Nothing could be further from the truth. I became ashamed and embarrassed; however, I still tried to maintain my role as pastor. I refused to get help. I found myself sinking deeper and deeper into depression. The burden was getting too heavy to bear. At one of my lowest points, I decided to confide in my spiritual mentor. Oh, what a man of God! He prayed with me, counseled me and directed me to a support group to help me deal with my problem. What a difference that made in my life.

Shortly afterwards, I decided to step down from the ministry for a year. I told the congregation that we were working on some family issues, and I needed space and time for proper healing. They agreed to give me a leave of absence from my position for as long as I needed.

I was accountable to three spiritually mature men during that year. They called me, spent time with me, prayed for me and confessed the Word of God over my life. They helped restore me to my proper place in the Body of Christ.

Now, I preach with compassion and passion to those who are struggling with sin. I don't preach from a judgmental attitude. I see others as God saw me. I believe this is why God allowed this congregation to grow as it has. Yes, I am back in ministry full force, and life has never been better. But things would never have turned around for me if I didn't confess my sin and reach out for help.

Luther's Advice:

Even if you are a believer, you have the potential to fall. If you do, go to mature brothers in the Lord for restoration. They aren't the restorers, but they can lead you to the One Who has power to restore. We all need help sometime, even those of us who love God with all of our hearts.

Thought Provokers

What was Luther's struggle?

Why do you think Luther initially refused to get help?

How did his refusal to get help negatively impact his life?

What do you think could have happened if the congregation found out about Luther's situation before he got help?

Do you think Luther made a wise decision in stepping down from the ministry for one year? Why or why not?

How did becoming accountable to other men help Luther?

Can you relate to Luther? Explain.

Do you think pastors (or men in leadership) would have a hard time being accountable to other men? Why or why not?

Chapter Six

Cedric is a thirty-four-year-old unemployed man. Prior to "his incident," he was a police officer. Things were going well on the force, and a promotion was in his future.

For the last two years, Cedric worked odd jobs: raking leaves, cutting grass, assisting construction workers, etc. He shared that it is difficult for him to obtain employment in his small hometown, and he hasn't moved because he has just enough income to provide for his necessities.

Cedric feels trapped in a "no-win" situation. He shares his story with the hope that someone would be encouraged.

Cedric Speaks:

As far back as I could remember, I always dreamt about becoming a police officer. My mom bought me police cars, toy pistols, cop uniforms and the entire gear so I could impersonate the role. I imagined myself catching the bad guys, rescuing the innocent and making this world a better place. I even visualized obtaining respect because of my uniform. I saw others recognizing my authority, and to me, authority was very important. After high school, my thoughts were no longer imaginations; the opportunity arose for me to live them out. I enrolled in the academy to fulfill my life-long dream. I was excited.

The time finally arrived for me to receive my first uniforms. I remembered smelling my uniforms and caressing my guns as if they were the most prized possessions in the world. To me, they were. I could barely wait for my first day of active duty. I told myself I would be the best cop ever.

I found myself stimulated by my job. I loved the excitement, especially of the chase. I volunteered to work long hours because I seemed so fulfilled while on duty. Any time I struggled in my personal life, I took it out on the criminals. I treated them rougher and talked to them harsher. They deserved it, and it was all covered in the line of duty. I even noticed the respect I had on the streets. When I rode by in my squad car, other vehicles cleared the path for me. They recognized my authority. I finally arrived. My role of a police officer gave me my due respect (by the majority anyway).

I remained on the force three years before I met my wife. Elaine was a fellow police officer, and she was smart as a whip. She relocated from California, and she was always ready for action. Elaine could intimidate any man who came across her path. She intrigued me, both professionally and personally.

I finally got the nerve to ask Elaine out. She didn't want any part of that because she didn't want to mix business with pleasure. I continued to ask her out until she finally consented. We had a whirlwind romance and married within six weeks of our first date.

After Elaine became my wife, I felt she needed to make a few changes. Even though she intrigued me, I wanted her to start acting more feminine. I complained about her hair, clothing, lack of make-up, etc. I told her she needed to put a feminine pep in her step, especially after business hours. I also wanted her to develop a more submissive attitude. At times, she intimidated me with her words, and I really didn't like that. Initially, Elaine resisted my requests, but after my continual nagging, she complied. She had bouts of acting feminine then she would relapse into her old behaviors. This infuriated me.

One winter night, after an extremely hectic day on the beat, I came home and found Elaine in sweat pants. I knew this should not have bothered me, but I told her a million times I wanted her looking more feminine when I came home. Unexpectedly, something took hold of me, and I slapped Elaine on the right side of her face with all the force I had. My action floored Elaine! It was like I shocked her, surprised her and scared her all in one blow. She ran out of the room in tears. I ran behind Elaine, crying that I didn't know what came over me. I begged for forgiveness and promised never to do anything of that sort again. She walked around the house for two weeks without saying a word to me. During that time, I bought her flowers, cards, gifts, and did chores, hoping to get back in her good graces. She finally let her wall down and started to trust me again.

Everything was lovely after that. I did my best to emulate the perfect husband. I was still angry about the way Elaine carried herself, but to avoid confrontations, I chugged a few beers. Part of me felt like Elaine disrespected my manhood. I knew she was a talented police officer, but she didn't have to flaunt that at home. She never openly did anything to disrespect me, but I had a gnawing suspicion that she inwardly felt she was a better police officer than I was. I needed her in her place, especially in our home. Anyway, these thoughts raged within me, but I hid them. I made sarcastic remarks to Elaine, but I always covered them with laughter. I felt the furnace getting hotter and hotter, but I concealed my feelings. Within, I was a steaming kettle, ready to explode.

Eight months after that little physical bout, I came home after having a few too many beers. Again, I found Elaine in sweat pants, and I immediately started cursing and throwing things. I held things in long enough, and it was time for complete and total change. I told Elaine that I was the only man in the house, and I wanted her in dresses when she wasn't on duty. She whimpered, went into our bedroom and locked the door behind her. For some reason, this made me furious. I pulled out my gun and started shooting the lock. I yelled her name, but there was no answer. After a brief shooting spree, I opened the door. There I saw Elaine, drenched in blood. Thank God, I didn't kill her. Two of the bullets hit her, one in the leg and the other one in the chest. I immediately called 9-1-1 and told them the situation. I told them it was an accident. After the paramedics arrived at the scene, they called the local police. They read me my rights, handcuffed me and hauled me off to jail (just as I had done to so many others in the line of duty).

Elaine's family refused to allow me to see her after the incident. They said Elaine never wanted to see me again. She recovered nicely; however, she has a limp in her left leg. (That's what someone told me.)

I spent years in prison because of this. Never in my life did I think anything like this could happen to me. A cop turned inmate. What a commentary. After my release, I never got back on track. I kept hurt, anger, shame, embarrassment, guilt and grief bottled up within me. I still hadn't dealt with my feelings. I just want to forget. To top it all off, I received divorce papers from Elaine after I got out of prison. I didn't contest the divorce. I knew I had it coming.

Now I sit before you, a broken man who has lost all hope, a man with a faded dream. An ex-cop turned ex-inmate. My pain is intense. I don't know how to escape it. I try to ignore it. At least my mind is freer during the day. The night hours still plague me. I keep reliving that night in my mind. A moment of rage changed my entire life. Boy, what a waste.

Cedric's Advice:

I knew I had an explosive temper, but I never thought it would come to this. I allowed my outbursts to run rampant without keeping them in check. As you can see, my rage ended up destroying my life. I'm not trying to tell you what to do because my life is in a shamble. All I can say is learn from my mistakes so you won't end up a broken man. Not only did I destroy my life, I also chipped away at someone else's life. Take it from me, it's not worth it. Get help before you or someone you love become a statistic.

Thought Provokers

What issues were Cedric dealing with?

Do you think Elaine's appearance was the cause of Cedric's anger? Explain.

How did Cedric deal with his anger?

How did Cedric's behaviors conflict with his occupation?

Cedric feels that he is in a "no-win" situation. What advice would you give him?

Can you relate to Cedric? Explain.

What are some other unhealthy ways men deal with their anger?

Chapter Seven

Mr. Young is an attractive seventy-year-old gentleman. He looks much younger than his age. He is very distinguished, and he has a deep dimple in his chin that makes you want to stare at it for hours. He is 6" 1", and his posture is very erect. His mannerisms display that he has been properly trained in etiquette. He warmly invited me into his study as we prepared for the interview.

As I looked around his home, I saw that Mr. Young was a collector of portraits. Most of his portraits consisted of scenes of soldiers. I took a few minutes to study the portraits, trying to determine what they revealed about this man of distinction.

Mr. Young agreed to talk about an intimate part of his life, a part he still holds dear. You see, Mr. Young is a widower.

Mr. Young Speaks:

I usually don't allow strangers in my home; however, you came highly recommended by a close friend. She was insistent that I take part in your study of men. Reluctantly, I agreed. (Mr. Young sits back in his leather chair and takes a few minutes to gather his thoughts.)

1954. Oh, what an extraordinary year that was for me. It was spring, and I felt that the world was mine to conquer. I worked as an apprentice for a local physician, and my work brought me great satisfaction. I wanted to learn everything I could about becoming a general practitioner. I devoted myself to my work, and my mentor continuously stroked me for my progress. He told me he saw future success for me.

Because I put in long hours with my mentor, I had little time for anything else. I wanted to stay focused, and I felt I couldn't afford any distractions. When people thought of the best general practitioner in my state, I wanted them to think of me (back then, I considered that a big vision).

Things continuously progressed as I planned. I worked hard, didn't play and worked hard again. During one of my busy days, a young lady walked into the practice, looking like a model from anybody's runway. She had long wavy hair, long legs and skin of perfection. There were a lot of other qualities I noticed, but I won't go into that (he smiles). She extended her hand and introduced herself to me. That was a monumental moment, forever etched in my mind. She informed me that she came to see my mentor. I smiled sheepishly and offered to walk her to my mentor's office.

Upon leaving her presence, I tried to focus on my work. Because I wanted to catch quick glimpses of her, I made several excuses to enter my mentor's office. During the last interruption, my mentor lifted his left eyebrow (as he usually did when he was serious), and I knew that meant no more interruptions. By the way, the young lady's name was Martha.

When Martha left the premises, I wanted to follow her home. After about thirty minutes of work, I could stand it no longer. I had to find out about this Martha. I sheepishly knocked on my mentor's door. In that moment of time, I felt like a child getting ready to ask for his father's car (a brand new car at that). Anyway, I got up the nerve to ask my mentor about Martha. He chuckled and said that she was his niece, and she would be staying with him for a few months. I tried to hide my excitement about the news. I knew I would see Martha again. I rushed out of his office and hurried back to work. I heard chuckles from my mentor's office as I scurried around, trying to contain my excitement.

A week passed before I saw Martha again (in the flesh that is, I saw her daily in my mind). I pulled my mentor aside and asked him was it all right for me to ask Martha out for a soda pop. He told me

Martha had to make that decision. When I asked her, she charmingly accepted.

Martha and I spent many hours together. I tried to stay focused on my work, but being with Martha became more important to me. I worked all day and found time in the late evenings to spend with Martha. She was so delightful. I enjoyed her company immensely. We dated for a few months then I asked Martha to marry me. It was so ironic. A man who was so single-minded before Martha became so divided after Martha. I didn't want to let her get away. We did marry, in the winter of that year, the year of 1954.

Martha and I had tremendous times together. During our marriage, we accomplished most of our goals. I completed my schooling and apprenticeship and became a general practitioner. Martha became a nurse. We enjoyed working and playing together. We traveled extensively, even abroad. We had many friends, attended many parties and enjoyed being with our families. Martha was my best friend. Never once did I desire another woman. I was so fulfilled with my Martha.

1999. A year that turned my world upside down. My darling Martha received a diagnosis of cancer. When she received the diagnosis, it didn't seem real. It felt like a cruel joke being played on April Fool's Day. She cried, and I cried. We both vowed to beat this thing; we refused to succumb to the news.

Months passed. I watched Martha get smaller and smaller and grow weaker and weaker. She tried to maintain her zest for life, but that was fading rapidly. I sat day by day, watching Martha slowly die. As she faded away, parts of me died with her. Oh how I loved that woman.

The evident finally happened. Martha died in my arms approximately forty-five years after I married her. (Tears rolled down Mr. Young's cheeks.) My lover, my best friend, my wife passed from this side and slipped into eternity. Her death devastated me. That day, I experienced a pain so great that I wanted to die right beside her. (He pauses for several moments.) My Martha, the only woman I ever loved, was gone.

As I examine my life, I realize how blessed I was. I experienced what many young men never experience: true love. I cherish the memories of my Martha. I haven't shown interest in another woman since Martha's death. I don't believe I could ever find someone to love like I loved her. At times, I still cry. I miss her embrace, her scent and her smile. I miss everything about her. She was (and still is) a big part of me.

Mr. Young's Advice:

Finding true love is a rarity these days. If you ever find it, cherish it with your whole heart. Show that special someone you love her. Treat her like a queen. Do your best to make her happy. Just remember, once she is gone, she is gone forever. If you do all you can while she is with you, you will never have regrets. You'll cherish the memories you made together.

Thought Provokers

Why is Mr. Young in pain?

Explain what you think Mr. Young lost as a result of his wife's death.

How is his wife's death affecting him?

What advice would you give Mr. Young?

Can you relate to Mr. Young? Explain.

If you are in a relationship, are there things you would do differently if you knew your mate received a life-threatening diagnosis? Explain.

Chapter Eight

Wondo, age twenty-nine, is a native of Africa but has been in the United States for the last three years. His accent is very distinct, and he pronounces his words deliberately to make sure he is not misunderstood. Wondo stands approximately 5'5", and he is medium built. He admits he is trying to learn the culture of America, which is drastically different from the culture of his native land.

Wondo agreed to tell of his struggles, hoping to help other men.

Wondo Speaks:

First of all, I feel honored to live in the United States of America. Since childhood, we heard stories about "the land of the free." Our elders told us there was a land where you could succeed regardless of your race, family history or economic status. As children, we longed to one day be a part of such a great country. I always told myself that my divine powers would lead me to this country if I believed hard enough. To my amazement, the divine led me here, to the land of the free.

I have no family here in the United States. My family from Africa had connections and arranged for me to stay with a family in North Carolina. I had a great opportunity, and to me, it was heaven.

I was very apprehensive when I first arrived in this country. I spoke English well, but I have a strong African accent so I had to repeat myself constantly so people could understand me. That made me self-conscious. My dress was very colorful (as it was in my country), and I noticed I was out of touch with the young men of my age group. This too made me self-conscious. We respected our elders, and I never fathomed speaking in a loud tone to a man of age. The women had servant attitudes (in a respectful way), and our elders stressed that you had to work hard to survive. It's amusing now, but the first time I saw things contrary to my value system, I wanted to run back to Africa.

About a year after my arrival, one of my American friends invited me to go to a club. I didn't really know what a club was, but I decided to attend just for the comradery. As I entered the club, I saw lights flashing, heard music booming, glanced hips swaying and eyed drinks flowing. I was always a good dancer so that part never bothered me. My comrade insisted that I get on the floor and show the crowd something. I swayed with the music, demonstrating my African moves. They were quite incredible if I must say so myself. I became an instant hit. As I left the club that night, I had five telephone numbers from five American sisters.

Week in and week out, I attended the club. I made many friends and finally found a place where I seemed to fit. One Saturday night, one of my comrades pulled me aside and said he wanted to talk to me. We went outside, near the back of the club. He had a pipe in his hand, a funny glass-looking pipe, and he told me it was a form of magic. He said he had a "magic rock," and it could show me things my ancestors never thought of. Until that time, I drank a little beer here and there, but I never went pass that. But that night, I looked good and felt fine, so I decided that a little "magic" could only enhance things. That was my first experience with crack cocaine. My comrade was right. That first hit made me feel more powerful, more confident, and more vibrant.

I didn't use crack anymore for at least a month, until one Saturday night. That night before we got our party groove on, a group of guys came by and laid the "magic rocks" on the table. We intended to go to the club after getting lit, but we ended up spending the entire night with "a little magic."

From there, my life took a downward spiral. I became addicted to the point that I spent all of my money on drugs. To support my habit, I stole from my American family. They didn't know what was going on with me. They questioned me about things, and I lied to cover every situation. I finally got tired of the hassle and moved in with one of my dealers. The agreement was to sell for him, and he would give me the necessities, including my "magic rock." I really indulged then. I lost twenty pounds in two weeks. I looked like a light pole with extremities. I became irritable, moody and depressed. My self-respect plummeted. I found myself in a web of lies and deceit and really didn't realize how I got there. I did things I never thought I would ever do. To make matters worse, I cut in on my dealer's profit. His boys beat me severely on several occasions. I finally left there and entered a homeless shelter. It was there that I met Lorenzo.

Lorenzo was a young man, approximately twenty-six years old. I met him because he conducted classes with some of the residents in the shelter. He shared that he had been in recovery for one year. I never met anyone who talked so openly about his experience with the "magic rock." Lorenzo shared how it took him to his lowest depths. He discussed some of the hideous things he did to get "a little magic." Unashamed, he admitted hitting rock bottom. (That phrase rang in my ears.) He ended his story by telling us of his experience with an addiction treatment facility and Narcotics Anonymous. Lorenzo said those things saved his life. He admitted that he was still struggling in some areas, but he was clean and sober. He invited anyone who had a problem with alcohol and drugs to come talk to him after the session.

I found myself drawn to Lorenzo. Not so much because I wanted to talk to him, I was just so low that I hated what I had become. When I approached him, he gave me a strong, manly hug. He acted as if I were a long, lost family member. He talked to me and got some information from me. He promised to get back with me by next week. (Sure you're right. I thought to myself. I figured I would never see him again.)

The next week, Lorenzo returned just as he promised. Not only did he return, he brought an appointment date for me to enter a treatment facility. He told me that it was out-of-state, but the room was ready and waiting for me if I wanted help. Since I had nothing to lose, I went.

I spent three months in a treatment facility in Georgia, and it changed my life. I experienced unconditional love from strangers (staff and residents). My self-esteem improved significantly, and I identified and worked towards accomplishing my goals. After completing the program, I returned to North Carolina, but in a different living environment and around different people. I am gainfully employed, and I am very active in Narcotics Anonymous. I feel like a new man. I can now say what Lorenzo said in one of his sessions: I am still struggling in some areas, but at least I'm clean and sober.

Wondo's Advice:

Experimenting with drugs is no joke. Anyone can get caught in the trap. I tried them to increase my confidence and ended up losing my self-respect. Drugs took me further than I wanted to go, had me doing things I never thought I would do and paying a price I never thought I would pay. If you haven't tried drugs, don't. If you're addicted, get help. If you're foolish enough to contend with the "magic rock" (or any drug), you will come out the loser every time.

Thought Provokers

What issues were Wondo dealing with?

Why do you think Wondo tried crack? List other reasons people try drugs.

List some things Wondo experienced after becoming addicted to crack.

Why do you think Wondo decided to get help?

What advice would you give Wondo?

Can you identify with Wondo? Explain.

If you had a friend who was experimenting with drugs, what would you do?

Chapter Nine

Harold, a thirty-year-old truck driver, admits he harbors rage. He is handsome, yet he keeps his baseball cap pulled over his eyes. He speaks with a baritone voice but looks to the ground when you engage him in conversation. He decided to share his story with the readers of this book.

Harold Speaks:

Women! Who needs them? We men do, and it makes me mad that we need them like we do. Yeah, society tells us to lead, support our families, work hard and be good providers. But where does all of that get you? With a lying, cheating, conniving woman. That's where it got me anyway.

Let me back up a few years. Tommy and I were best friends since freshmen in high school. When you saw me, you saw Tommy. When you saw Tommy, you saw me. Everybody said we were like Siamese twins. We were about the same size and even exchanged clothes and shoes on a few occasions. (Now you know that's close.) Anyway, when we left high school, we went to the same college and hung out with the same friends. We even double-dated. He dated Irene, and I datedSharon. The four of us did many things together. We enjoyed each other. When I had a problem with Sharon, I discussed it with Tommy. When he had a problem with Irene, he discussed it with me. We were boys like that.

Sharon (my girl) was the outgoing, cheerful type. She loved being the center of attention. She had a shape that people noticed, and she knew how to draw attention to herself in the most charming, yet unobtrusive way. I didn't mind because I knew Sharon loved me, and I really adored her. We made the perfect match.

Three years into our relationship, things changed. Sharon distanced herself from me. She said she needed space to find herself. Being the type man I am, I thought it was a female thing. I discussed it with Tommy, and he felt the same way. He told me women went through moods, and sensitive men knew how to give them space without feeling intimidated. That sounded good to me, so I gave Sharon space.

As time passed, Sharon and I spent less time with Tommy and Irene. We also spent less time with each other. I didn't hang out as much with Tommy because he always seemed busy with appointments, practices and engagements. I started to get concerned, but I figured given time and space, everything would work itself out.

After graduation from college, I continued to see Sharon; however, she grew more distant and preoccupied. Because I loved her, I asked her to talk to me about our relationship. She would shrug her shoulders and give me lame excuses, never addressing any serious issues.

I finally got tired of the drama. I told Sharon I was going out-of-town for the weekend to spend time with my family. I had to get away to get my head together.

Strangely, Sharon was very attentive to me that night. She hadn't been that way with me in some time. She cooked me dinner at her place. We watched a movie, and we kissed goodnight. This was the Sharon I fell in love with, the old Sharon. I hated to leave, but since I already planned the trip, I felt I had to go. I told her I would return on the following Monday. With that, I was off to my condo to pack my bags. While packing, I realized I left my camcorder at Sharon's. I wanted to get it before she went to bed.

When I arrived at Sharon's door, things seemed strange. All the lights were out. That part wasn't strange. The strange part was that Tommy's truck was in her driveway. Why would his truck be parked there at this time of night? All type of thoughts raced through my mind. I rebuked myself for being suspicious. There was a legitimate reason for this. Maybe Tommy, Irene and Sharon went somewhere, and Sharon forgot to tell me so I used my key and unlocked the door.

As I entered, I slowly looked around Sharon's apartment. My heart raced uncontrollably. My eyes moved slowly throughout the familiar atmosphere. Candles were burning. Soft, alluring jazz music was playing (my favorite), and I thought I heard voices coming from Sharon's upstairs bedroom. I stood stunned for a few minutes. No, I told myself. This could not be. I remained frozen in time until my mind convinced me to go upstairs.

I found myself slowly tipping up the stairs. Every step became heavier and heavier, and my breathing became shallow. I felt like I was in a horror movie, anticipating the most heart-wrenching moment of my life. Part of me wanted to turn back, but a force compelled me to continue. As I got to Sharon's bedroom, I slightly pushed the door. To my amazement, I found Sharon in the lingerie I bought her, all wrapped around my best friend! I yelled, and they both looked at me startled.

I turned and ran out of that place like a wounded gazelle. Tommy ran after me in some silk boxers, and inwardly, I wanted to snatch them off his behind. Through angry tears, I got into my truck, sped out of the driveway and locked myself in my condo. My phone rang and rang. From the caller ID, I could tell it was coming from Sharon's apartment. I took my phone off of the hook. My cell phone started to ring. The numbers alternated from Sharon's apartment and Tommy's cell phone. I turned my phone off. Well, you can guess what type night I had. I cried myself to sleep. I slept for an hour, woke up and cried some more. Why didn't I see this? How long had it been going on? Did Irene know? What a fool I've been. My best friend with my girl, nothing can cut you any deeper than that.

I refused all calls from Tommy and Sharon. After the initial shock, I left town. I decided that relocating would be the best thing for me. I couldn't take a chance of running into either of them.

This happened some years ago, and I am still reeling from the pain. I really don't know how to get past this. Right now, I think I hate all women. Who needs them? We men do, but it still makes me mad that we need them like we do.

Harold's Advice:

I don't really have any advice at this point. I'm still hurting too badly. It seems I can't get that picture out of my mind, Tommy wrapped around my girl, and my girl wrapped around Tommy. All I can say is keep your eyes open and remain watchful. Don't get hurt like I did.

Thought Provokers

How was Harold betrayed?

Do you think Harold played any part in his betrayal? Explain.

If you were in Harold's position, what would you have done after you found out about Sharon and Tommy?

What advice can you give Harold?

Can you identify with Harold? Explain.

Do you think a friendship or relationship could survive a betrayal like this? Explain.

Chapter Ten

Sidney plays for a semi-pro football team. He is well-known and well-liked in his hometown. They see him as a hero.

Sidney has always advanced in football, ever since junior high school. If he ever got his hands on the ball, there was no stopping him. He spent many hours reviewing game tapes, trying to find ways to improve his game. He made his parents proud.

He decided to tell his story. Sidney wants other men to make better choices than he did. He hopes his story will save someone's life.

Sidney Speaks:

I'm twenty-four years old, and I should be in the prime of my life. Notice I said "should." I play football, and it's my passion. I know the game inside and out. I have great coaches and teammates, and we all seem to get along. In my hometown, they tell me I'm a superstar. I find myself getting preferential treatment at home: free burgers, the best seats, discounts and a whole host of other things. My parents beam every time they see me.

The girls around home always chased me. I must admit, I allowed a few of them to catch me. I really didn't want a serious relationship. I wanted a honey here and a honey there, just someone present when I felt a little lonely.

Things went on like that for a couple of years: the fanfare, preferential treatment, the popularity. I thought I was invincible (how deceived I was). Anyway, to me, the world was treating me mighty good.

One cold and chilly day, I called my physician to get a check-up. I was feeling pretty good; however, one of my uncles found out that he had prostate cancer about two weeks prior. I didn't want the same thing to happen to me.

After one of my hottest games, I came home and tried to relax. It was approximately a week after my appointment. As I listened to my messages, a nurse's voice came on the answering machine. She said I needed to set an appointment to see my physician. That was strange. Never before had my physician wanted to see me. Well, I waited until the next day to make the call. I decided not to worry about it. It was probably something minor.

On the day of the appointment, I got up extremely early. Surprisingly, I was a little apprehensive about going to see my physician. Could it be cancer? No, I told myself. I'm too young for that. I tried to muster up courage, but I felt fear beginning to grip me. I reminded myself of my abilities and skills. I tried to focus on how I beat many odds. I knew I was being silly for entertaining fear, and I told myself fear had to go! As I talked to myself, I hurried to get dressed while forcing the harassing thoughts to the back of my mind. After dressing, I rushed out the house. I don't know why I was in such a hurry; I guess I was trying to get away from me. I got in my car and started driving. I drove around until it was time for my doctor's appointment.

By the time I arrived at my physician's office, I had worked myself into a frenzy. (Can you believe it? A big, bad football star feeling like a frightened, lost puppy.) I could tell that my physician detected my nervousness. He was very cordial with me then he invited me into his office and directed me towards one of his leather chairs. He spoke in a soft, monotone voice and informed me that he had the results of my blood work. I intently listened as he proceeded. He whispered as if he didn't want to hurt my feelings. "Mr. Harris, (it sounded like he prolonged my name) your test results are positive for HIV." What did he mean HIV? I told him there was definitely a mistake. Didn't he know I was a football player (one of the best)? Didn't he know I had a great future before me? He definitely had to have my test results mixed up with someone else's. He invited me to get a second opinion. I got up and left his office. The doctor's words terrified me.

I figured my physician was a small-town doctor, and surely, he made a mistake. After finding a physician in a bigger city, I had the same physical performed. A week after my appointment, his nurse left a message on my answering machine. She said the doctor needed to see me personally. I went in for the appointment and came out with the same disturbing news. I was HIV positive.

Right now, I'm the only one, outside of my physicians and their nurses, who knows. What am I going to do? I am too young to die. How could I be so careless? The honeys I chose were fine. They couldn't have been HIV positive. Unfortunately, somebody was.

Well, I found out about this six months ago. I am too embarrassed to tell anyone. It will ruin my career, and it will definitely ruin my name. How will my parents respond? For now, it's my secret and burden. And a heavy burden it is.

Sidney's Advice:

Running through women may seem cool, but the price you pay is deadly. It's not cool when the doctor diagnoses you with an incurable disease. Think about your actions before you act. Thinking later may cost your life.

Thought Provokers

What is Sidney's secret?

How do you think Sidney felt when he found out that he was HIV positive?

Why do you think Sidney won't tell anyone about his diagnosis?

What would you do if you were Sidney?

Can you relate to Sidney? Explain.

What are some risky behaviors people engage in that make them susceptible to contracting the HIV virus?

List some myths people have about individuals who are HIV positive.

Chapter Eleven

Lawrence is a manager at one of the local pizza parlors. He makes one of the best pizzas your lips would ever touch. He's the only person I know who can flip the dough, dance a step and catch the dough without missing a beat. It's a joy to watch him work.

Lawrence recently celebrated five years of marriage. He's forty-two, and his wife is thirty-two. They've tried to conceive since their first year in marriage, but unfortunately, Jeanie continues to have miscarriages. Lawrence is usually a cheerful person, but this situation has taken a toll on him. After four miscarriages, Lawrence's disappointment flows through his words. He puts on his best face for his wife because he doesn't want to hurt her feelings.

Lawrence shares his heart about longing to become a father. He tells what he does to get through some of his pain.

Lawrence Speaks:

I'm a decent man. I have good morals, work hard and provide for my wife. I can't give her the finest things in life, but what is mine is hers. Lately, I've been working on showing her my sensitive side. That has really been a job.

Jeanie and I discussed having children before we got married. We both wanted children; we didn't care about the gender. I love children and so does Jeanie. She works at a daycare, and she's one of the best teachers there. Her love for children shows in her work.

Immediately after we got married, Jeanie got pregnant. We were so excited. I think we practically had the entire baby room furnished within four weeks of finding out. We picked out names of girls and boys, eagerly awaiting our new arrival. Eight weeks into the pregnancy, Jeanie complained of stomachaches. One Friday night, I rushed her to the emergency room. After hours of waiting, the staff told us Jeanie had a miscarriage. Upon receiving the news, we both had heart-felt crying sessions.

Thereafter, I was extra supportive of Jeanie. As difficult as it was, Jeanie tried to put her happy face back on. I saw through the masquerade; I knew she was hurting. I was too. Since I was the man, I portrayed strength. I spent more time at work to ease the pain, and Jeanie started journaling.

After our first pregnancy, Jeanie became pregnant three other times. She never carried the baby past two months. Each miscarriage chipped away at our self-esteems as well as our marriage. When it came time to become intimate, Jeanie complained of headaches. Every day, she had a new complaint.

As her husband, I tried to support her. Even though I spent more time at work, I complimented her and did things for her. Jeanie pulled further and further away from me (emotionally and spiritually). She criticized herself, and then she criticized me. I knew what the problem was, but I didn't know what to do. I had no solutions.

After awhile, our intimate life was non-existent. Jeanie said she wouldn't risk losing another baby, something she desperately wanted.

At that point, I became angry with God. I looked around at the men who were having babies from different women then neglecting the children. Why were they allowed to have children, and we weren't? I also questioned my manhood. Was there something wrong with me? I even questioned Jeanie's womanhood. Accusing thoughts bombarded my mind day and night. I had to do something. I was losing myself, and I was losing my wife.

I finally contacted a counselor and set an appointment for me and Jeanie. I told Jeanie we had to go to save our marriage. We had a wonderful counselor. She helped us work through our grief as well as our anger towards God. We set small goals regarding regaining intimacy in our marriage. It took months, but we now feel closer than ever before.

It's still hard talking about losing a child, especially when you desperately want children. Right now, Jeanie and I are hopeful. We decided that if we don't have children by the time Jeanie is thirty-seven, we would adopt. We both feel very comfortable with this decision.

Lawrence's Advice:

Please don't take fatherhood for granted. It is a gift, one not given to every man. If you are one of the fortunate ones, cherish it.

Thought Provokers

What was Lawrence dealing with?

How did he initially handle things?

List how things worsened when Lawrence and Jeanie failed to discuss things.

What do you think was the breaking point for Lawrence?

What would you have done if you were in Lawrence's position?

Can you identify with Lawrence? Explain.

What would you do if you wanted a child and thought you couldn't have one?

Chapter Twelve

Travis was a seventeen-year-old basketball star in his senior year of high school. He was looking forward to going to college. He hadn't decided which college he wanted to attend because he had so many scouts looking at him. Travis was hoping to get a basketball scholarship that would pay for his college tuition.

He decided to tell us about his unfulfilled dreams.

Travis Speaks:

I was the athletic type. I experimented with many sports but found my niche in basketball; I excelled in that sport. As far as my health, I exercised daily and ate three balanced meals every day. Even though my physical health excelled, my mental health lagged behind. I remembered stats and plays, but I was never good in school. I didn't have to worry though; people did my homework for me.

I scooted through classes, never really understanding the material. My teachers liked me, and I was especially nice to them. Some of them gave me grades I didn't deserve. They knew the athletic talent I had and didn't want to do anything to interfere with the school's basketball star.

I must admit, I enjoyed attending school. I wasn't into learning, but the socialization was great. I especially enjoyed gym class. It was a time for me to sport what I knew. It was my time to shine. I demonstrated my physical abilities, and often left my gym mates full of jealousy.

One afternoon, I was on my way with some of the guys to play a little street ball. I didn't usually do this, but being bored, I needed a challenge. On our way to the court, we approached a four-way stop. My partner looked left and right, and then proceeded. A SUV (that was speeding in the area) ran the stop sign. It crashed into the car that we were in and totaled it. The other three boys had cuts and bruises all over their bodies, but I experienced something different.

Thrown out the car, I landed on the nearby sidewalk. To make matters worse, I couldn't move. One of the boys told me to keep still, and he would call the ambulance. The ambulance, fire truck and police car arrived on the scene about the same time. I remembered them lifting me into the ambulance, and then I blacked out. When I came to, I was in a critical care unit. I had tubes running to and from every part of my body. I was too numb to comprehend what was going on at the time.

Through groggy eyes, I saw my parents hovering over me. I tried to speak but slurred my words. I guess the nurses gave me medicines to ease the pain. My parents encouraged me to get some rest, and they promised to talk to me later. I remained in bed, but I had no other choice, I still couldn't move. Moments later, I drifted into a deep sleep.

The next day, my parents returned to my room. Dad took the lead, and I could tell they were upset. Dad informed me that I had a broken back, and the doctors didn't think I would ever play basketball again. Tears rolled down my cheeks. I was at a loss for words. My mom just rubbed my arm and cried. My dad turned his back and walked towards the door. I could tell he was crying too. It was the most painful moment of my life. Not only did I lose my basketball career, I had nothing to fall back on.

Now I'm in a rehab center. They work with me every day, but the progress is slow. I feel a lot of physical pain, and much of the time, I'm heavily medicated. I'm trying not to give up, but I'm losing heart pretty quickly. For the first two months, I had a lot of visitors. That is slowing down too. I guess people start to forget after a while. I promised myself I was going to get a tutor when I get back up to par. I don't want to be ignorant and lame. I guess I idolized the sport too much. I had all of my eggs in one basket, and they all got crushed. I'm trying to recoup, but I know it will be a long process. Right now, I'm barely hanging on.

Travis' Advice:

I want to speak to the young brothers. Get an education; always have something to fall back on. Sports are good, but have a back-up plan if that doesn't pan out. And no matter what life deals you, hang in there. Sooner or later, you'll get dealt a better hand (if you don't give up).

Thought Provokers

What was Travis' tragedy?

Do you think he was prepared for this? Explain.

List some things Travis may have lost because of his injury.

What advice would you give Travis?

Can you relate to Travis? Explain.

Have you ever experienced an injury (or illness) that changed the course of your life? Explain.

Interview Questions

Tell me about yourself (be as detailed as possible).

What is your motto about men expressing hurts?

Where did you get this message (friends, parents, teachers, preachers)?

Have you ever been hurt emotionally?

Let's talk about a situation in which you were hurt. (Identify the situation, your thoughts about the situation, your feelings about the situation, and your actions because of the situation).

Do you think this hurt has impacted your life? In other words, how are you different because of this hurt?

Do you think this hurt is hindering you from going further in any area of your life? Explain.

Do you think this hurt has helped you mature or become a better person? Explain.

Is there anything you wish you would have done differently regarding this hurt? Explain.

What advice would you give to a man who is experiencing hurt or has experienced a hurt similar to this?

Additional Comments:

Important Note: In order to obtain information regarding men's hurts, I devised a ten-question interview tool. This tool can be used in the hands of a trained professional.

www.ingramcontent.com/pod-product-compliance
Lightning Source LLC
Chambersburg PA
CBHW051947280526
45789CB00009B/3199